THE FABER LIBRARY

OF ILLUMINATED MANUSCRIPTS

edited by Walter Oakeshott

The Benedictional of St. Ethelwold

THE FABER LIBRARY OF ILLUMINATED MANUSCRIPTS

edited by Walter Oakeshott

THE BENEDICTIONAL OF ST. ETHELWOLD
Francis Wormald

THE PARISIAN MINIATURIST HONORÉ
Eric G. Millar

THE GREAT LAMBETH BIBLE
C. R. Dodwell

THE ROHAN BOOK OF HOURS
Jean Porcher

THE VIENNA GENESIS
E. Wellesz

A FIFTEENTH CENTURY PLUTARCH
Charles Mitchell

THE BENEDICTIONAL OF ST. ETHELWOLD

with an introduction and notes

by

FRANCIS WORMALD

FABER AND FABER LIMITED
24 Russell Square London

FIRST PUBLISHED IN MCMLIX
BY FABER AND FABER LIMITED
24 RUSSELL SQUARE LONDON WC1
PRINTED IN GREAT BRITAIN
BY WESTERN PRINTING SERVICES LTD, BRISTOL
COLOUR PLATES MADE AND PRINTED
BY FINE ART ENGRAVERS LTD, GUILDFORD

To

PROFESSOR OTTO HOMBURGER

with many thanks

Introduction

One of the greatest periods in the history of English medieval art is that associated with the revival of Benedictine monasticism in the second half of the tenth century. A great series of illuminated MSS. dating from about A.D. 960 to the Norman Conquest in 1066 bears witness to the extraordinary artistic activity during this period. Besides the important kings Athelstan, 925–939, and Edgar, 959–975, three ecclesiastics stand out as pioneers in the work of ecclesiastical reform: Dunstan, Archbishop of Canterbury, 960–988, Ethelwold, bishop of Winchester 963–984, and Oswald, bishop of Worcester 961–992, being after 972 also Archbishop of York. This revival of the religious life expanded rapidly and abbeys were founded or refounded all over Southern England. An almost immediate consequence of this was an increased production of books, some of them richly decorated. Amongst them one of the most splendid examples is the Benedictional of St. Ethelwold, bishop of Winchester, now Additional MS. 49598 in the British Museum.

Unlike many illuminated MSS. something is known of its origin. The information is given in a Latin poem written in golden capitals at the beginning of the book, and is worth quoting in full. This is a translation of it:—

'A bishop, the great Ethelwold, whom the Lord had made patron of Winchester, ordered a certain monk subject to him to write the present book. Knowing well how to preserve Christ's fleecy lambs from the malignant art of the devil; illustrious, venerable and benign he desires also to render as a good steward full fruit to God, when the Judge who sifts the acts of the whole world, what each has done, shall come and give such reward as they deserve: to the just eternal life and punishment to the unrighteous. He commanded also to be made in this book many frames well adorned and filled with various figures decorated with numerous beautiful colours and with gold. This book the Boanerges aforesaid caused to be indited for himself and in order that he might be able to sanctify the people of the Saviour by means of it and pour forth holy prayers to God for the flock committed to him, and that he may lose no lambkin of the fold, but may be able to say with joy, "Lo I present to thee myself and the children whom thou didst give me to keep; by thy aid not one of them has the fierce ravening wolf snatched away, but we stand together and desire to receive abiding life and to enjoy it in the heavens with the supreme sovereign whose members we are, who by right is the head and salvation of those baptized in the clear-sounding name of the Father, and of the Son, and of the Holy Ghost, so that, if they wander not astray, but hold the faith, and by their deeds also perform the commands of salvation and repel all heresy from their hearts, ever striving to overcome the evil of sin; they may be joined to the Lord in heaven without end. May Christ the Saviour, who is the good king of the world, mercifully grant this to all who are sprinkled with holy baptism; and to the great father who ordered this book to be written may He grant an eternal kingdom above. Let all who look upon this book pray always that after the term of the flesh I may abide in heaven—Godeman the scribe, as a suppliant, earnestly asks this".'

Bombastic as it is, this inscription is extremely valuable. It tells us that it was written for Ethelwold, bishop of Winchester, for his personal use, by one Godeman. Some conclusions may be drawn from this.

A certain amount of information exists about St. Ethelwold. He was born, probably of noble parentage, in Winchester. At an early age he went to the court of King Athelstan where he attracted the latter's notice. He was then ordained and later received the monastic habit from St. Dunstan at Glastonbury in Somerset. Some time later Ethelwold wished to go abroad in order to complete his monastic training in one of the newly reformed monasteries on the Continent. His intention was frustrated by the action of the Queen who persuaded King Edred to forbid his departure in the interests of the country. About 954 Ethelwold left Glastonbury and with some companions went to the refounded monastry at Abingdon where he became abbot. Within a short time he had organized the monastic life there and planned for new buildings. This refounding of Abingdon was only the first of the many reformations which now began. The great period of late Anglo-Saxon monasticism really begins with the accession of Edgar as the King of the whole country in 959. In the following year Dunstan became Archbishop of Canterbury and three years later in 963 Ethelwold was consecrated bishop and appointed to the see of Winchester. Almost immediately the energetic bishop reformed the two important Winchester monasteries: the Old Minster which was attached to the cathedral, and the New Minster which later became Hyde Abbey. He did this by removing the non-monastic clerics and substituting monks in their place. Under the year 964 the the Anglo-Saxon Chronicle says 'In this year King Edgar drove out the priests from the Old Minster and from the New Minster of Winchester, and from Chertsey, and from Milton Abbas (Dorset) and planted monks in those churches.' This was, however, only a beginning and shortly afterwards Ethelwold was refounding the great East Anglian abbeys of Ely and Peterborough and founding Thorney. His efforts, though in the end successful, were not always achieved without opposition, as on the occasion when the Winchester 'clerics' nearly succeeded in poisoning their bishop.

A Benedictional is essentially a book made for the bishop's own use. It contains a series ot solemn blessings to be said by the bishop over the congregation during the Mass. These blessings which were pronounced during the most solemn part of the service seem to have been regarded as a preparation for the Communion. No one but a bishop could give them. In consequence a book containing them would be almost certainly made for him or for an ecclesiastical establishment closely connected with him. The texts of these blessings varied in accordance with the day or season on which they were to be said in rather the same way in which collects vary. The actual blessing was made with considerable ceremony, the congregation being specially exhorted to prepare itself for this solemn act. Though never a part of the Roman use benedictions were used throughout the Middle Ages.

Few Benedictionals are as sumptuous as St. Ethelwold's and they rarely contain elaborate decoration. Another English example from the same period as Ethelwold exists, however, and is now in the Bibliothèque Nationale in Paris (fonds lat. 987). It contains fine illuminated borders and it resembles our MS. in many respects. Another magnificent MS. is the so-called 'Benedictional' of Archbishop Robert of Jumièges, now MS. 369 (Y.7) in the Bibliothèque Municipale in Rouen. Actually this MS. is really a Pontifical made for a bishop of Winchester, possibly Ethelwold himself, since it is contemporary with the Ethelwold benedictional and with that in Paris.

Nothing is known of the fate of the Benedictional after St. Ethelwold's death. It presumably remained amongst the treasures of a cathedral or abbey connected with the saint. There is a small piece of evidence that this was Hyde Abbey at Winchester, or, as it was known in Anglo-Saxon times before its removal to Hyde in 1110, the New Minster. This evidence is provided by some bits of documents used at some time to reinforce the binding of the MS. These documents seem to have come from the office of the treasurer of an ecclesiastical establishment. Between folios 26 and 27 of the MS. enough of one of these is visible for it to be identified as a list of relics. In this reference is made to the shrines in which the relics were preserved. Three of these shrines indicate quite clearly that the list comes from Hyde Abbey. After the name of the relic there are notes saying 'in scrinio barn', 'in scrinio valen', and 'in scrinio gr'. They can be interpreted as follows:— 'in scrinio barnabe', in the shrine of St. Barnabas, 'in scrinio Valentini', in the shrine of St. Valentine, and 'in scrinio greco', in the Greek shrine. It is known from other sources that there were important shrines of SS. Barnabas and Valentine at Hyde Abbey, and a reliquary known as the Greek shrine has been there since Anglo-Saxon times. The date of these fragments is fifteenth century. When the MS. was reinforced with them is not known, but it indicates that the MS. remained at Winchester and was probably preserved at Hyde Abbey.

The Winchester monasteries were dissolved in the sixteenth century, Hyde in 1538, and the Cathedral Priory or the Old Minster in 1539. It was presumably at this time that the Benedictional lost any sumptuous binding that it may have had. Its wonderful condition suggests that up till then it must have been preserved amongst the treasures of its owners. Whether it remained at Winchester cannot be shown. In the late seventeenth century it received its present leather binding. By 1720 the MS. had passed into the possession of William Cavendish, second Duke of Devonshire to whom it had been given by General Hatton Compton. Compton was appointed Lieutenant of the Tower in 1715 and died early in 1741. How he came by the book is unknown. Robert Harley, Earl of Oxford, an avid book collector, tried to get it for his collection in 1720, but the Duke would not part with it; and so until 1957 it remained in the library of the Dukes of Devonshire.

The dates between which the MS. was made are certain, being governed by the episcopacy of St. Ethelwold at Winchester between 963 and 984. Within these limits it is impossible to be more precise. At the same time the reference to miracles performed recently at the shrine of St. Swithun in the blessing for his day suggests that the book was put together after 971 when that saint was translated. A date between 971 and 984 would be quite acceptable. Godeman the scribe has not been identified with certainty. It is likely that he was the Winchester monk who afterwards became abbot of Thorney in Lincolnshire. In which of the Winchester monasteries the MS. was written is not clear. There is some evidence for identifying Godeman with a monk of the Old Minster, since his name is found in the *Liber Vitae* of Hyde Abbey amongst the brethren of the Old Minster.

As it exists today the MS. consists of 119 leaves of vellum measuring 11½ inches in height and 8½ inches in width. There are usually 19 lines of writing to a page, and the ruling was made by the impression of a sharp-pointed instrument. The ruling of the boundary lines of the text-space is reinforced by pencil lines which are apparently contemporary with the writing of the MS. The script used for the text throughout is a large and handsome Carolingian minuscule, which occasionally looks a little uncertain as if the scribe might be more at home with the Insular type of writing. Large square capitals are used for some of the headings (Pl. 5). Sometimes uncials and rustic capitals are found (Plates 6,7). The dedicatory poem is written throughout in golden rustic capitals.

Godeman's Carolingian minuscule (Pl. 8) is a very early example of the use of this famous script in England. Before the period of tenth-century monastic reform and for at least fifty years after it the normal script employed by English scribes was based upon the Insular script which had grown up in the British Isles at the end of the sixth century and continued to develop during the intervening centuries. The introduction of Carolingian minuscule into English scriptoria is a symptom of the new monasticism with its imitation and adaptation of continental habits, and its desire to follow Carolingian models. Two other MSS. show in their script really striking resemblances to the Benedictional of St. Ethelwold. First is the other English Benedictional in the Bibliothèque Nationale which has already been referred to (B.N. fonds lat. 987) and which is also textually closely related to our MS. Second is a fragment of a Gospel Lectionary, now in the Arundel MSS. in the College of Arms, London (Arundel MS. XXII, ff.84, 85). Both these MSS. are so close to the Benedictional of St. Ethelwold that even if they were not written by Godeman himself they were clearly all written in the same scriptorium. Two other English MSS. also show a very similar type of large Carolingian minuscule. The first is a Psalter now in the British Museum (Harley MS. 2904) which was probably written at Ramsey in Huntingdonshire towards the end of the tenth century. Its script is very close to the MSS. just mentioned. The second is another Winchester MS., the splendidly sumptuous copy of King Edgar's charter of 966 to the New Minster at Winchester. This magnificent document which is in codex form is written throughout in golden Carolingian minuscule. It is preceded by a frontispiece showing the king with Christ in Majesty, St. Mary and St. Peter. Whether the charter is exactly contemporary with the date it bears is uncertain, but it is probably not very much later than 966. The New Minster Charter with the Benedictional of St. Ethelwold are, therefore, amongst the earliest as well as the most important documents for the history of late Anglo-Saxon illumination. Another charter (B.M. Augustus II. 33), a grant from King Eadwig dated 956, is also written in large Carolingian minuscule. Here again it is likely that the date of the actual script is a little later.

The decoration of the Benedictional is, however, its crowning glory. This consists of a series of twenty-eight full-page miniatures, nineteen pages of decorative frames either rectangular or arched, one historiated initial within a decorative frame and one historiated initial alone. Originally there were probably fifteen more miniatures and two more pages with borders. The missing miniatures include a group at the beginning of the MS. which is now incomplete. There were probably twelve of them and what they represented will be discussed below. Besides this group at the beginning there are leaves missing between folios 20 and 21, 105 and 106, and 107 and 108. They must have contained miniatures of the Massacre of the Innocents, the Nativity of the Virgin, and St. Michael.

Each miniature within the body of the text is placed within a decorative frame, i.e. the 'circi' of the dedicatory poem. This frame is either rectangular or arched. Opposite the miniature is a page where the opening words of the blessing are written in golden capitals enclosed in a frame which matches that on the opposite page (Plates 6, 7). The choice of feasts to receive miniatures and decoration of this kind was naturally governed by their liturgical importance. St. Swithun of Winchester and St. Etheldreda of Ely whose abbey Ethelwold refounded are the only English saints honoured in this way. As befits a Benedictine MS., St. Benedict has also a miniature. Here is a list of the miniatures in the MS.

1. F.1. The choir of Confessors. Seven crowned saints. Three of them are identified by inscriptions as SS. Gregory the Great, Benedict and Cuthbert.

2, 3. Ff.1b,2. The choir of Virgins standing under arches. Amongst them Our Lady, St. Mary Magdalene and St. Etheldreda can be identified.

4–7. Ff.2b–4. The Twelve Apostles arranged in threes.

8. F.5b. The First Sunday in Advent. The Annunciation, in a rectangular frame.

9. F.9b. The Third Sunday in Advent. The Second Coming, in an arched frame. Plate 3.

10. F.15b. Christmas Day. The Nativity, in a rectangular frame.

11. F.17b. St. Stephen (26 Dec.) The Martyrdom of St. Stephen, in an arched frame.

12. F.19b. St. John the Evangelist (27 Dec.) St. John seated writing his gospel inspired by his symbol, the eagle, in a rectangular frame.

13. F.22b. Octave of Christmas (1 Jan.) The miniature is divided horizontally into two parts. Above is the Virgin seated on a couch with Christ as a child. Below are three men seated talking on a low bench. This scene probably refers to the Infancy of Christ and to the passage in St. Luke's Gospel (2. 52) which forms part of the Gospel of the day: 'And Jesus increased in wisdom and stature, and in favour with God and man.' A rectangular frame.

14,15. The Epiphany (Jan 6.) Two miniatures in rectangular frames: F24b. The Adoration of the Magi, F.25, The Baptism of Christ.

16. F.34b. The Purification of the Virgin (2 Feb.) The Presentation in the Temple, in an arched frame. Plate 4.

17. F.45b. Palm Sunday. The Entry into Jerusalem, in a rectangular frame.

18. F.51b. Easter Sunday. The Women at the Sepulchre, in a rectangular frame.

19. F.56b. The First Sunday after Easter (Low Sunday). Doubting Thomas, in an arched frame.

20. F.64b. Ascension Day. The Ascension of Christ, in a rectangular frame.
21. F.67b. Whit Sunday. The Descent of the Holy Ghost, in an arched frame.
22. F.90b. St. Etheldreda (23 June). St. Etheldreda standing, Plate 6.
Facing on F.91 is the opening of the blessing with an initial O in which is represented Christ blessing, Plate 7.
23. F.92b. The Nativity of St. John the Baptist (24 June). The miniature is divided horizontally . Above is St. Elizabeth lying on a bed with the infant St. John the Baptist in a cradle nearby. Below Zacharias writes on a tablet 'iohannes est nomen' (His name is John). Before him sit two men and two women.
24. F.95b. St. Peter (30 June). The Martyrdom of St. Peter, in a rectangular frame.
25. F.97b. St. Swithun (2 July). The saint is dressed in Mass vestments. Arched frame.
26. F.99b. Translation of St. Benedict (11 July). The saint seated and dressed in Mass vestments holds a book on his knee with his right hand and a crown in his left hand. Rectangular frame.
27. F.102b. The Assumption of the Virgin. (15 August). The Death of the Virgin, under an arched frame.
28. F.118b. Dedication of the Church. A bishop, possibly St. Ethelwold, pronouncing the episcopal blessing. Plate 8.

As was said above there are some miniatures missing from the beginning of the book. These preliminary miniatures formed a unit with number 1–7 of the existing ones. What survives today are only part of the Choir of Confessors, No. 1, the Choir of Virgins, Nos. 2, 3, and the series of Apostles, Nos. 4 to 7. It is obvious that other Choirs must have formed part of what was lost. In reconstructing the missing portion one is greatly assisted by two miniatures in a rather earlier MS. from Winchester: the Athelstan Psalter, now Cotton MS. Galba A.XVIII in the British Museum. These are found on folios 2b and 21 of that MS. Both show Christ surrounded by various choirs. In the first Christ is shown in a mandorla with three instruments of the Passion: the spear, the sponge and the cross. The miniature is divided into four horizontal zones each one containing a choir: the choir of Angels, the choir of Prophets, the choir of Patriarchs and the choir of Apostles. In the second Christ is shown in Majesty holding a cross, surrounded by the three choirs of Martyrs, Confessors and Virgins. From these two miniatures it is possible to suggest that the miniatures at the beginning of the Benedictional were arranged as follows:— i, Christ in Majesty, ii, iii choir of Angels, iv, v choir of Prophets, vi, vii choir of Patriarchs, viii, ix choir of Apostles, x, xi choir of Martyrs with xii the first page of the choir of Confessors. This would mean that six leaves of miniatures are now missing. Whether these particular miniatures were actually derived from the Athelstan Psalter is uncertain, but there is some evidence for thinking that they may have been. On the other hand the Carolingian miniaturists certainly knew a composition showing Christ in Majesty adored by various choirs. There is a fragment of a Sacramentary in the Bibliothèque Nationale in Paris (fonds lat.1141) which has two miniatures at the beginning of the Sanctus. On one is Christ in Majesty, on the other the choirs of Angels, Apostles, Martyrs, Confessors and Virgins in adoration. The composition is, however, very different from those of either the Benedictional or the Athelstan Psalter.

All the miniatures and the decorated pages are framed with leafy ornament of an extremely characteristic type. It is often called 'Winchester' acanthus, the name being derived from the Benedictional of St. Ethelwold and the other MSS. related to it. These frames are formed by a kind of gold trellis work over which climbs the leafy ornament. In structure this trellis work in the rectangular frames consists of a rectangle punctuated at the four corners and in the centre of each side by round bosses. These bosses provide the focal points from which the leafy ornament springs. The leaves which are painted in colours shoot out, under and over the golden frame work, producing a kaleidoscope-like interlace of tossing leaves. Gold being neutral in tone enables the leaves to behave in what appears to be quite independent fashion. The frame thus acts as a kind of atmospheric support to the dancing leaves. In the case of the round-headed miniatures (Plates 1,3,4) the leaf work seems rather more strictly confined to the space within the gold border, but at the corners there are the same tightly curled leafy bosses which lighten the general appearance of the frame.

Both the frames and the leafy ornament were introduced into English illumination from the Carolingian art of the Continent, and they came from different schools of MS. decoration; yet their combination in the form just described seems to be wholly English. The frames with their round corner bosses are clearly derived from the Franco-Saxon illumination of Northern France. Some Franco-Saxon MSS. even fill these bosses with leaf work, but to find really comparable exuberant leaves one must look at such MSS. as the ninth century Drogo Sacramentary from Metz in the Bibliothèque Nationale in Paris. Even there the leaves are less tempestuous in their behaviour. In one place in the Benedictional of St. Ethelwold the influence of Franco-Saxon ornament can be seen. This is the miniature of the Presentation in the Temple (Plate 4) where at the crown of the arched frame there is a roundel of gold interlace.

In the figures of the miniatures of the Benedictional we see some of the most splendid examples of late Anglo-Saxon illumination. As in the ornament the figure style is directly derived from Carolingian art. The technique is an elaborate one. First the outline of the figure was quite simply drawn in red. This under drawing may be seen clearly in the miniature of the dedication of the Church (Plate 8). Colour was then laid on in broad areas and worked up with a rather darker shade. Finally thin dark and light lines were added which provide a scintillating network of darkness and light all over the surface. This glittering effect is very much enhanced by the introduction into the outline of the drapery of a system of elaborate folds executed in quick flickering strokes which became one of the hall-marks of late Anglo-Saxon drawing. These folds may be very clearly seen in such figures as the Apostles (Plate 2) or on the veils of St. Etheldreda (Plate 6) and of the Virgin (Plate 4). Diagonal folds of drapery are also most characteristic such as those on the figures of the Apostles and the seated Christ in Majesty (Plate 2, 5).

Although the modelling of the faces is worked up with great care, the figures themselves have very little solidity in them. Their vitality is gained not from their integral firmness of form, but from the kaleidoscope of light and dark lines which plays over the surface of the drapery. Even such a figure as that of St. Etheldreda, (Plate 6,) which at first sight seems to have a certain weight, shows nothing of the bodily structure beneath her splendid garments. Her life comes from the flickering folds of her cloak and from her long-fingered hands which stretch out with the sensitiveness of antennae.

If one of the figures of the Apostles on Plate 2 is analysed exactly the same kind of surface activity can be seen. The three Apostles in this plate do not stand on the ground under the great arch forming their frame. They glide as it were over the surface, the legs and feet covering the ground, but like shadows skimming over rather than resting on its surface. Certain anatomical features such as the rotundity of the stomach or the joint of a knee are indicated, but they are symbols rather than representations of reality.

This illusionism is particularly marked in the relationship of figure to frame. Unlike so many borders these serve as it were as an anchorage rather than as a confinement. Figures may ride beyond its confines and yet a connection remains between them and the frame that holds them.

Though certain suggestions may be made about the Carolingian sources of the figure style in late Anglo-Saxon illumination its ultimate origin remains unsolved. It need not necessarily have been a single source, since as has already been noticed in the ornament, the English illuminators were perfectly capable of combining several styles into one of their own, and in doing so transforming them into something quite new. Owing to the researches of Professor Otto Homburger it is known that iconographically some of the miniatures in the Benedictional are connected with the so-called Metz School of Carolingian ivory carving. In the ornament also a relationship to Metz MSS. has already been noticed. The figure style of the earlier of the late Anglo-Saxon MSS. shows considerable influence of the MSS. connected with the Court School of Charlemagne, often known as the Ada Group. This influence is seen very clearly in such figures as the seated Christ in Majesty in the initial for the blessing on Trinity Sunday (Plate 5) which can be compared with an ivory probably representing Philosophy or Divine Wisdom now in the Metropolitan Museum in New York. The crumpled veils on the heads of the Virgin and St. Etheldreda are extraordinarily close to that on the head of the ivory Philosophy. Indeed it would not be surprising if one day that ivory were shown to be English. At the same time the curious cloudy backgrounds of the Benedictional are not found in the Court School of Charlemagne (Ada Group). They derive ultimately from Late Antique illusionism and may come directly from the Palace School and the Metz and Rheims MSS. of the ninth century (Plate 2).

These eclectic characteristics of late Anglo-Saxon illumination make it probable that it was a mixture of styles rather than the result of a single model. In this mixture it is possible that ivory carving as well as illumination may have played an important part. It must be remembered that not only the iconography, but something of the style of the Metz ivories may be detected in the Benedictional of St. Ethelwold. At the same time the most formative element in the figure style was closely connected with the Court School of Charlemagne. Not only the diagonal folds of the drapery and the network of light and shade strokes recall these MSS., but the statuesque figures of the Apostles (c.f. Plate 2) and even some of the colour should be compared with the evangelists in the Ada Gospels in Trier or the Gospel Book in the British Museum, Harley MS. 2788.

The Benedictional of St. Ethelwold stands at the head of a long line of magnificent illuminated MSS. made in Southern England in the century between the accession of St. Ethelwold to the see of Winchester and the Battle of Hastings. It was not the first English illuminated MS. to be decorated in the new style. The life of St. Cuthbert presented by King Athelstan to Durham probably in 937 and the additional miniatures in the Athelstan Psalter, B.M. Cotton MS. Galba A.XVIII already show the influence of Carolingian art. Closer to it in time are the New Minster Charter already mentioned and the Pontifical of Archbishop Robert of Jumièges in Rouen. All these MSS. have some claim to have been made at Winchester, but it would be a mistake to assign all MSS. in this style to Winchester alone. The style seems to have been common to the newly reformed Benedictine houses. Amongst these were certainly the abbeys of Christ Church and St. Augustine's at Canterbury. Bury St. Edmunds and Peterborough also produced fine books at a later date.

During the century which saw the flourishing of this school of illumination there were many different manifestations of it as well as a clear stylistic development. One of the most significant was the perfection of a wonderful outline drawing technique. Even in the Benedictional we already have indications of an extraordinary mastery of outline. It can be seen most easily in the figures drawn in outline only in the miniature for the dedication of a church (Plate 8), but it is even more characteristically displayed in the veils of the figures of the Virgin and St. Etheldreda (Plates 4, 8) where the well-known staccato strokes can be seen. Another significant stylistic change was the rise in importance of the influence of the Rheims style of illumination. At first as in the New Minster Charter and the Benedictional of St. Ethelwold the most important element is that of the Court School of Charlemagne. Gradually the illumination of the Rheims style, probably due to the direct influence of the Utrecht Psalter, gains the ascendancy. This is accompanied by a much softer treatment of folds and draperies. At the same time the leafy ornament begins to develop still further its habits of stretching and intertwining itself. Instead of being rather short the leaves extend themselves into long stalks ending in a twirl of foliage. Yet in this process of emaciation of the leaf work there is no fundamental change from what was already happening to Carolingian foliage in the Benedictional of St. Ethelwold. The tempo has increased. The convolutions are more violent, but the seed of this tumultuous interlace lies already in the frames of the Benedictional.

PLATE 1

THE CHOIR OF VIRGINS

F.1b. $8\frac{7}{8}'' \times 7\frac{1}{2}''$ (22.5 × 19.0 cm.)

The Blessed Virgin with six other female saints standing on rocky ground. All wear crowns and have blue haloes. Above is an angel holding a scroll. This miniature forms part of a series representing the Choirs of Heaven which originally decorated the first leaves of the MS. A number of these miniatures are now lost, see p. 12. The three chief figures hold books in their hands.

C

PLATE 2

ST. PETER WITH TWO APOSTLES

F.4. 9″ × 6⅞″ (22.8 × 17.5 cm.)

St. Peter is in the middle and is shown with the tonsure. He holds a cross and a pair of keys in his right hand and a large book in his left. The Apostle on the left has two books and the one on the right one book. Under the large arch are two angels holding a scroll. Below them are two flying angels holding golden books. Typical 'Winchester' leaf-work can be seen on the capitals and the bases of the columns. Note the diagonal folds of drapery, particularly on the figure on the left. This miniature is the last of the set of preliminary pictures at the beginning of the MS., see p. 12 which consisted of a Christ in Majesty, the Choirs of Heaven and the Apostles.

PLATE 3

THE SECOND COMING OF CHRIST

F.9b. 9½″ × 7½″ (24.1 × 19.0 cm.)

This miniature, which precedes the benedictions for the Third Sunday in Advent, has been described as representing the Ascending Christ. The text of the benedictions make it clear that the Second Coming is intended. The subject which is a rare one was inspired by St. Mark xiii. 26, 27. 'And then shall they see the Son of man coming in the clouds with great power and glory. And then shall he send his angels, and shall gather together his elect,' and also from Revelation i. 7. 'Behold, he cometh with clouds; and every eye shall see him, and they also which pierced him.' Christ is shown in a mandorla holding over His right shoulder a crossed staff. In His left hand is a book. On the robes over the right thigh is written 'Rex Regum et Dominus Dominantium' (King of Kings and Lord of Lords) referring to Revelation xix, 16. 'And he hath on his vesture and on his thigh a name written, King of Kings and Lord of Lords.' In the sky are angels, three of whom carry the Spear, the Sponge, and the Cross. It will be remembered that the same three emblems of the Passion are found in B.M. Cotton MS. Galba A.XVIII, f.2b.

PLATE 4

THE PRESENTATION IN THE TEMPLE

F.34b. $8\frac{1}{2}'' \times 7''$ (21.5 × 17.7 cm.)

On the left are the Blessed Virgin, a woman attendant, and behind them St. Joseph holding up the offering of a pair of turtle-doves, see St. Luke ii. 24. The Virgin holds Christ up over an altar draped with a golden cloth towards Simeon who, with Anna the prophetess, stands on the right. Above the Hand of God issues from a blue cloud. Note the roundel of gold interlaces in the centre of the arch. This is derived from Franco-Saxon and not from Anglo-Saxon illumination.

PLATE 5

CHRIST IN MAJESTY

F.70. $7\frac{3}{4}'' \times 5\frac{5}{8}''$ (19.8 × 14.3 cm.)

The figure is placed within an initial O which decorates the first benediction for the First Sunday after Pentecost. The opening words are 'Omnipotens Trinitas Vnus et Verus Deus. Pater, et Filius et Spiritus Sanctus', Almighty Trinity, the One True God, Father, Son and Holy Spirit. This figure, which should be compared with the Carolinngia ivory plaque with a figure of Philosophy in the Metropolitan Museum in New York, shows very strongly the influence of Carolingian illumination; particularly that of the so-called Ada Group associated with the Court of Charlemagne. It is a particularly characteristic representative of the 'First Style' of late Anglo-Saxon illumination before it was strongly influenced by such MSS. as the Utrecht Psalter.

D

PLATE 6

ST. ETHELDREDA

F.90b. 9″ × 7″ (22.8 × 18.0 cm.)

St. Etheldreda, abbess of Ely, died in A.D. 679. She is holding a book in her right hand and a flowering branch in her left hand. The inscription written in gold uncials reads 'Imago Sanctæ Ætheldrythæ Abbatissae ac Perpetuae Virginis', the representation of St. Etheldreda abbess and perpetual virgin. She was buried at Ely where she had been abbess and her shrine was there until the Dissolution of the Monasteries. Fragments of it may still be seen at Ely. St. Ethelwold may have had some veneration for her. He refounded her abbey between A.D. 963 and 969. The drawing of the saint's veil is very characteristic, and the borders are particularly splendid examples of 'Winchester' leaf-work.

Ima
go
SCE
ÆTHEL
ABB
PETUE
UIRGIN

PLATE 7

INITIAL O WITH CHRIST BLESSING

F.91. 9″ × 7″ (22.8 × 18.0 cm.)

This letter decorates the opening words of the blessing for the feast of St. Etheldreda. This page stands opposite that containing the figure of St. Etheldreda (Pl. 6).

MPS
UNU S ET
ÆTER NUS
DEUS

PLATE 8

A BISHOP PRONOUNCING THE BENEDICTION

F.118b. $7\frac{3}{4}'' \times 5\frac{7}{8}''$ (19.8 × 14.9 cm.)

This miniature is placed before the blessing to be said at the dedication of a church. At the top of the page may be seen three lines of the Carolingian minuscule in which the main body of the text of the MS. is written. The miniature itself is technically interesting since it shows the outline drawing as the fully painted technique. It is improbable that the miniature was left unfinished and it is much more likely that the architecture and the figures were intended from the beginning to be uncoloured in order to emphasize the importance of the chief figure, see BM. Arundel MS. 155, fol. 133.

The scene shows a bishop dressed in Mass vestments standing under a baldachino in front of an altar upon which are paten and chalice. A group of ecclesiastics are standing in front of him. One holds up a golden book, the Benedictional, from which the bishop reads. In a higher register, possibly denoting a gallery or a pew, are the heads of a number of lay persons including a lady. Whether this scene actually represents St. Ethelwold pronouncing the blessing at the dedication of the cathedral of Winchester in 980 cannot be certain. It would in any case be dangerous to assume that this miniature gives any certain indication of the appearance of the Saxon cathedral of Winchester. In a poem describing Ethelwold's cathedral reference is made to a weathercock. Two appear in this miniature; the one on the left is damaged, but is clearly part of the original and may be the one mentioned. It appears to have been golden.

repleri . ut cum eis caelestis spon
si thalamum ualeatis ingre
di · Quod ipse ·